INSTANT PICNIC FUN

si frankel

Association Press • New York

INSTANT PICNIC FUN

VIRGINIA MUSSELMAN

INSTANT PICNIC FUN

Publisher's stock number: 1645
Library of Congress catalog card number: 67-14589

PRINTED IN THE UNITED STATES OF AMERICA

This book is dedicated to my mother
CAROLINE WATKINS MUSSELMAN
affectionately known as
"Miss Carrie"
whose loving heart and joy in living warms everyone
around her and gives a special shine to every
day and holiday.

AUTHOR'S PREFACE

During my years as director of program activities for the National Recreation Association (now the National Recreation and Park Association), scarcely a day went by without a letter from some person or agency planning a picnic and asking for help. It was very evident that while picnic information could be found by digging into game collections in libraries, few people had the time or the inclination to make a research project out of picnic planning. Few people needed that much information. Few people, unless they were in the business, were willing to purchase a large, expensive book in order to meet a one-time need.

In some communities, public recreation agencies have come to the rescue with mimeographed manuals, but these are usually available only locally (Reading, Pennsylvania; Louisville, Kentucky; Chicago, Illinois; Berkeley, California; and Linden, New Jersey are only a few of the cities whose recreation agencies deserve special praise for such efforts).

7

What seemed to be most needed was a collection of old and new picnic activities—short enough to be used easily, simple enough not to require professional recreational training, interesting enough to stimulate their use, and inexpensive enough for most pocketbooks.

Some of the games and contests will be old favorites. Some may be new. In all of them, I have tried to give not only the directions for playing, but also what supplies will be needed. A tug-of-war just can't be run without a rope, but how many people know offhand how long or how thick that rope ought to be? And have you ever tried to find out? It's not easy!

Picnics, like plays, require "props." The smoother the picnic moves along, the more *somebody* has worked ahead of time, setting up the playing area and collecting the equipment. The supplies used in most of the activities in this book are easy to find and inexpensive to buy. Whenever possible, substitutes or variations have been suggested.

I have tried to keep the activities interesting, exciting, amusing and in good taste. Any contests requiring eating, for example, have been chosen carefully. Spills and smears can be wiped up, but a post-picnic tummy ache is not fun for parent or child. I have included a few old-time traditional contests, such as Hog Calling and Chicken Calling. They fit into some picnics and can be kept out of others. Directions for them are hard to locate in the more sophisticated game books. In our increasingly urban communities, many people have never heard of, or taken part in, such contests. Perhaps they will have a certain nostalgic value for the oldsters and be hilarious to their grandchildren.

Many picnic activities are games and contests useful also

for playground programs, camps and day camps, play days, school- and back-yard play. I hope that the readers of this book will use it for other events as well as for picnics.

I have not included traditional picnic activities such as the softball or baseball game and various track and field events. These can be added to any picnic plan, providing qualified leaders are available. The activities here are those that require very little, if any, previous training, and are therefore better fitted to be called INSTANT.

Most games have a long and honorable history. All over the world people play and enjoy games so similar that only the titles are different. With very few exceptions (basketball being one) games are not invented. They *evolve*. Each generation adds its own slight changes or adaptations, but the basic games remain. They are as old as the past, as new as the future.

Who knows who first thought of an egg-throwing contest, its modern version with ice cubes? Who first thought up the piñata? Who planned the first penny scramble? The first balloon-breaking contest? Rooster fight? All the hoop games? The potato race? I wish I knew! Whoever they were, they deserve the thanks of thousands of people, young and old, who have laughed and had picnic fun because of those games. If I have not given credit where credit is due, it has been through lack of information, not oversight. It is not intentional. I apologize, ask forgiveness, and say a sincere "Thank You, Whoever You Are"!

VIRGINIA MUSSELMAN
New York, New York

CONTENTS

SELECTOR CROSS-REFERENCE INDEX

Picnic activities and themes particularly suitable for various groups and suited to certain types of space are listed here by the number under which each appears in the book. In many instances, however, games and contests can be adapted or modified very easily to make them suitable for other groups or picnic settings.

Don't take this index as final. Use your own judgment. It's your picnic!

TYPE OF GROUP

All-Adult—1-9, 18, 21, 23, 24, 26, 28, 31-34, 37-45, 47-49, 51-66, 68-75.

All-Child—4, 6, 10-20, 22, 23, 27, 28, 30, 31, 33, 35-39, 41, 42, 44, 47, 49-51, 56, 58, 59, 63-65, 67, 71, 74, 75.

All-Boy—4, 6, 10-20, 22, 23, 25, 27-39, 41, 42, 47, 49-56, 58, 59, 63-67, 74.

All-Girl—4, 6, 10-19, 21, 23, 26-33, 36-43, 47, 49, 51, 56, 58, 59, 61, 63, 64, 74.

Average (100 or less)—1-45, 47-69.
Club, Church or Other Agency—1-45, 47-66, 68-71, 74, 75.
Community-Wide—1-45, 47-66, 68-71, 74, 75.
Family—1-4, 6, 10-12, 15, 17, 18, 23, 28, 33, 35, 37, 38, 41, 42, 49, 51, 56, 58, 59, 63, 64, 67, 71, 72-74.
Large (100 or more)—1-45, 47-66, 68-71, 74, 75.
Older Adults—1-9, 21, 23, 24, 28, 37, 38, 41-45, 48, 49, 51, 59-63, 68-70, 72-74.
Small (25 or less)—1-4, 6, 7, 10-13, 15-18, 21, 23, 28, 33, 37, 38, 41-45, 47-49, 51, 55-64, 67-74.
Teenagers—1-8, 17-19, 21, 23-28, 30-45, 47-56, 58-61, 63-66, 68-75.
Young Couples—1-8, 18, 21, 23, 24, 26, 28, 30, 32, 34, 37-45, 47-49, 51-64, 68-70, 72-75.

TYPE OF SPACE

Back Yard—1-7, 10-13, 15-19, 21-23, 28, 32-43, 45, 47, 48, 49, 51-59, 63, 64, 67-73.
Beach—1-4, 8, 10, 12, 13, 15-24, 27-42, 44, 47-71, 74.
Camp—1-8, 10-30, 32-39, 41, 42, 44, 45, 47-56, 58-72.
Indoor—1-9, 11, 15, 18, 19, 21, 23, 32, 34, 37-45, 49, 51, 56, 59, 63, 67, 68, 70-73.
Limited Space—1-15, 18, 19, 21, 23, 28, 32, 34, 35, 37-45, 48, 49, 51, 55-64, 67, 68, 70, 72, 73.
Parks and Playgrounds—1-45, 47-71, 75.
Plenty of Space—1-45, 47-71, 74, 75.

INSTANT PICNIC FUN

chapter 1

INSTANT

PICNIC PLANNING

BASICS

A picnic is probably the only recreation activity that can be
enjoyed by one person or by thousands. Its program can
range from deck-chair-and-hammock lounging to a complicated all-day and evening industrial affair with events for
all ages from five-year-old Fred to Fred's eighty-five-year-
old Grandpa. Picnic food can range from a sandwich and a
candy bar tucked into a coat pocket to a mammoth and
fabulous meal served by caterers to thousands. A picnic can
take place in the back yard or on the patio, or in a huge
amusement park rented for the purpose.

In between these extremes are the picnics which we are
more likely to be planning for. These also have a wide
range in size, but not impossibly wide. They include the
picnics that are just a bit bigger and more involved than the
everyday, family-only "Let's cook out tonight," yet not so
large and so complex as to require months of work by many
committees making complicated plans for entertainment,

18

transportation, lighting, and catering. This book will offer suggestions to make these occasions easy for the planners and good fun for the guests.

Not many people need detailed information on the big, industrial-size picnic. How many of us will ever cope with a picnic for thirty-five thousand men, women and children, such as a division of General Motors has conducted? How many of us will ever cope with the buying and serving of twenty-six hundred pounds of hot dogs devoured at a Delco Remy picnic, along with two hundred and fifty gallons of mustard? See RESOURCES for information on that kind of picnic.

Not many parents need help in the family-style picnic in the back yard or nearest picnic area. Public libraries are full of books on table, board, guessing and other limited-activity games for family fun. It's when someone says "Let's invite the neighbors," or when the children say "May we ask our classes?" that the picnic begins to become a project. Questions arise, too, when the civic club, the church, the PTA or other private or public agency decides to have a picnic and YOU get put on a committee. These are the challenging picnics, the ones that require some degree of planning: decisions concerning site, time, decorations, food, transportation, safety, and program.

We are an active people. Clubs, neighborhoods, churches, schools, and even whole communities enjoy getting together outdoors, eating together and playing together. Anything can be an excuse for a picnic: a birthday, a holiday, an anniversary, a reward for school work, a close of a season, or just "Isn't it fun to get together?"

Like any social event, the more work done ahead of

time, the smoother, the more "instant" the actual event. Also, the larger the picnic, the more pre-picnic help you will need in planning it. That's where sharing the work through committees is a good idea. A committee can consist of you and the next-door neighbor or a group of high-powered businessmen. For large community, church or other picnics, some group has to figure out expenses and set up a budget. Another group has to find the best place for the picnic. Still another must decide upon the games and contests, find judges, buy prizes, see that play areas are marked and that supplies needed are at hand.

None of these decisions can be made without first of all considering the picnic group. Who are they? How many? Do they know each other? What is the age range? How far do they have to come? What do they like to do? Site, food, games, prizes—they all depend upon the people.

Whatever the type of group, or the size and kind of picnic you are planning, it will involve the three picnic basics:

People · Eating · Program

Easy to remember! Their initials spell

P E P

SAFETY AND COMFORT

THE SITE

Selecting the site is a major first step in planning the picnic. Perhaps it's your own back yard or patio. Perhaps it's down on the beach. Perhaps in a nearby State park.

Perhaps it's a corner of a nearby amusement park. Before settling on any site, no matter how lovely, make a list and check off the things you must be sure about.

Here are some of the questions that must be answered, whether you invite your neighbors for a potluck picnic in the back yard, or take your family to the beach, or get your name placed on your club's committee for its annual affair, or are elected chairman of the Community Picnic for July 4.

Toilet facilities. Whether the picnic is in your own home or in a corner of a big amusement park that your company is renting, adequate toilet facilities must be available. Where can mother change baby's diaper? Where can Jane fix her hairdo and John wash the mustard off his fingers? Or the youngsters get out of their wet bathing suits?

Drinking water. No matter how many soft drinks are available, people will want a drink of water. If the picnic is a home or family affair, water can be cooled in the refrigerator or carried in a thermos. But if the folks are on the beach, or in a park, where can safe drinking water be found? If it's not there, it must be brought in. Try to find a site where drinking water is readily available.

Parking. Even if you've invited a fairly small number of friends and relatives, many of them will come by car. Is your driveway large enough to handle them? Or should you look for some other parking space? If the picnic is a large or fairly large affair for your club, or church, school, or community, parking space is required. It must be clearly marked and there must be enough of it. It should be fairly close, or some drop-off and pick-up area be provided, so that

older people and women with very young children are
saved a long walk. Direction signs should be put out to
guide drivers to the parking area.

   Game area. Any picnic except the very small affair where
lounging and eating are the major part of the program will
require an area large enough for races, games, stunts and
other activities. The size depends upon the number of
people and the activities they will take part in, or watch. A
community picnic may spread over the entire Village
Green or the local park. The program for it might include
a softball game, tennis games, horseshoes, and volleyball.
These all require special play areas.

   In general, all the activities in this book can fit nicely
into an open playing area of around 60 by 100 feet. When
ball games, hundred-yard dashes, and other track and field
events are planned, they will require additional space. This
playing area of 60 by 100 feet should be marked or roped
off, so as to leave it free for the activities. Spectator space
should be provided around it. Marking the field into
smaller sections—25 feet, 50 feet, 75 feet, 100 feet—will
make it easier to set up any of the special races and relays
described in this book.

COMFORT

   While folks are usually active on a picnic, they will need
places to sit down and rest, eat their lunch, or watch a race,
or cheer a stunt. What seating facilities are there: benches,
chairs, steps, pillows, grass? What about tables? Tables for
food, for sitting around with friends, for "resting" the lunch
basket or shopping bag, for holding a soft drink or cup of

coffee? Shade is important, too, for cooling off after active games.

Being able to see and to hear is necessary for comfort. For large picnics, a platform, public address system, and adequate lighting will make the difference between success and failure. A good emcee can make a happy picnic.

SAFETY

Don't take safety for granted! It's no fun to come down with a bad case of poison ivy a few days after the picnic. It's no fun to spend the day swatting flies or mosquitoes. Skinned knees and cut feet or hands caused by broken glass, or other litter in the playing area, can spoil the day for child and parents. A water area, no matter how small, is particularly dangerous for children unless someone watches over them. A child who wanders off into the woods can become lost and frighten both himself and those hunting for him. These and most hazards are prevented easily if they are foreseen.

Safety also is a factor in all the picnic activities. Too much exertion can be a hazard for adults not used to much physical activity. Old bones break easily. Older people should not take part in sack races, three-legged or other races where spills are almost inevitable. Sunburn from too much exposure can cause a miserable, sleepless night.

Always have a first aid kit handy and know how to use it. For large picnics, a first aid station should be set up, with a trained nurse in charge and a local doctor and hospital within telephone distance. It is also a good idea when planning a big picnic to notify the police department. Better be safe than sorry!

IF IT RAINS

Have a plan and tell folks about it. If the picnic is a small family-friend affair, tell the guests "Come, rain or shine!" and just move indoors. A picnic on the floor or around the fireplace can be lots of fun. The activities will have to be different, unless your indoor space is huge, but the picnickers won't care.

For larger picnics, decide ahead of time about what will be done in case of rain. Is indoor space nearby? If so, prepare an alternate plan. Move indoors and put that plan into operation. Perhaps it can include entertainment, such as a talent show, and several types of music. Singing together is a big part of such a program, but vary it with a combo, with folk songs, rounds, and "answer" songs.

If the crowd is too large for such a program change, or if indoor space is not available, make sure that people know ahead of time that the picnic will be postponed in case of rain and set another date. Sometimes the local radio station will make last-minute announcements of sudden changes in plans. It's up to you to alert them.

GATE CRASHERS

Maybe it has never happened to you, but gate crashers have been a real problem at some picnics. Here again, it is best to be ready for such an emergency by hoping it won't happen but knowing what to do if it does.

Teen-agers often ask parents not to be around when they have "the gang" in for a party or picnic. They say it spoils things, that parents don't trust them. Don't fall for this! It is asking for trouble. The youngsters are not old enough—or are too uncertain and too inexperienced—to handle what might be a bad situation.

Be on hand. Behind the scenes, perhaps, after you have met and greeted the young people, but be there. If part of the house is off limits to the picnic guests, say so and make it stick. If boys or girls show up uninvited, having heard the music or seen the lights, send them off with courtesy but firmness. And if the gate crashers become offensive or unruly, call the police.

At large picnics planned for specific groups—a club, school, church—the procedure should be somewhat the same. Members should have some sort of identification: a big badge, a red cap, a lei, a special hat. "Outsiders" should be greeted courteously, the event explained to them, and then requested politely to leave. Most of the time this is enough. Gate crashers are problems more at evening events than in the daytime, more at teen-age events than at those of other age groups.

DRINKING

Picnics can be spoiled by any guest who insists that alcoholic drinks are needed to make them go. The host and hostess of a small picnic at their own home or their personal picnic elsewhere can usually handle this problem with good natured firmness. Teen-age picnics sometimes include a boy who brings a bottle and offers it openly or surreptitiously to the others. This is another reason for parents to be on hand and quietly observant. They can take charge of the situation by saying "We don't allow liquor, Joe. I'll put your bottle on this shelf, and you can pick it up when you leave." Or make some other quiet indication of firm disapproval. Don't take any excuses or make any compromises at times like that. Again, it's up to the parents (or leaders) to get the teen-agers off the hook in a situation they might not be able to handle without losing face with their peers. Poise and tact are not characteristics of all young people.

PICNIC KITS

FAMILY-SIZE

What to carry as a picnic kit depends upon the number of people who will be using it and the kind of activities they will engage in. A kit for your family should contain the supplies and equipment suitable for all the members and for the sort of games you enjoy together. This equipment should also be suitable to the place where you're holding the picnic.

Such a kit for use by family or a small group might include some or all the items below, but tailor it to your own use and your group's likes and dislikes. Among popular items for family and small group picnics are:

Favorite toys (doll, teddy bear, stuffed toy)
Storybook (for small ones' nap time)
Table or board game, crossword puzzle, playing cards, for relaxed adults and teens
Softball and bat for informal ball play
Quoits or deck tennis rings
Rope (for a substitute net)
Balloons

Soft rubber ball
First aid kit

Add other useful items such as toasting forks, charcoal, outdoor grill. Also, don't forget small items that provide surprises or special events: paper plates for "sailing," plastic spoons used in races or contests involving food, lollipops for prizes, bean bags for throwing games. Any special activity, such as fishing, will require special gear and, in some cases, special clothing. Pick out whatever activities will be fun and then plan the picnic kit around them.

For Larger Groups

For a large picnic involving activities for a wide age range, you'll need more supplies. Basic equipment usually includes such items as:

4 volleyballs (for races and games as well as for volleyball)
1 set of horseshoes and stakes
25 burlap bags (for that sack race)
2 softballs (for the inevitable ball game)
2 softball bats
4 dozen clothespins (for relays)
Tug-of-War rope 2 inches by 25 feet
2 clothes lines about 50 feet long (for various contests, and for net substitutes)
10 or more newspapers (used to make "swatters" for races and contests)
A duffle bag (a good carrier for such supplies)

To such a Picnic Game Kit, you'll have to add all the items needed for any special games, races, relays and stunts, plus the necessary prizes. Items most often used in the activities in this book will include:

Plastic spoons	Bean bags
Broomsticks	Tin or paper plates
Potatoes	String
Paper bags	Balloons
Tin or paper cups	Sticks, canes
Burlap sacks	Lollipops
Hard candies	Clothespins

Use the Selector Cross-Reference Index to find activities suitable for your picnic. Make a list of all the items needed for them. You'll find it a good idea to group the items needed for each activity and keep them all together in a well-marked paper or plastic bag. It will save you time and that panicky feeling that you've forgotten something.

PUBLIC RECREATION AGENCY LOAN SERVICE

Don't buy any athletic supplies for a picnic until you have checked with your local recreation and/or park department. Most of them have picnic kits that you can borrow. Usually they're free (you pay for any replacements necessary) or cost only a small fee. Sometimes this amount is refunded when the kit is returned in good shape. The kits and other supplies provided by public agencies are mostly athletic. They will not supply the small, inexpensive items needed for most of the races and contests. These, plus the prizes, are your responsibility.

PRIZES

Three words are good to remember when deciding upon prizes:

SIMPLE · SUITABLE · SILLY

Whenever possible, avoid prizes of money and expensive articles. People come to a picnic to have fun. Too much competition can turn a friendly contest into a bitter battle when a big prize is at stake. It is much more fun for everyone if there are lots of prizes, all of them simple, suitable or silly.

Small children are easy. Prizes for their scrambles and other contests should be limited to small items such as:

Balloons	Lollipops
Bright new pennies	Bubble gum
Flags	Storybooks
Candy kisses	Candy bars

Toy counters in local novelty shops, five-and-dime stores and supermarkets often carry small items that children like. Stock up on them when you find them. They might not be available when you start looking for them.

If you decide to limit prizes to one type, such as balloons or candy bars, try to buy them wholesale. Figure out how many you'll need, add extras just in case, and then buy them by the box or gross. You'll save money. (This principle applies also to inexpensive prizes for adults, such as key rings, small flashlights and other novelties.)

A basic rule to remember in planning prizes for the Under-Sixes is EVERYBODY GETS A PRIZE. If you're using balloons, for example, the winner might get the only red one, but everybody else would also get a balloon. Small children don't understand losing. A balloon isn't really a prize to a small child. It's a symbol of belonging. It's "Look what I did! I was there, too!"

For the Slightly-Olders, bright, gay and inexpensive prizes might include such things as:

Rubber balls	Badges
Jacks	Jump ropes
Marbles	Kites
Comic books	Puzzles
Whistles	Novelty hats
Toy autos	Toy planes

Bright, gay prizes for teens and adults add a fiesta look to the picnic and to the winners. Crepe paper leis, bright South Sea Island or cowboy hats, jockey caps, headbands, bandannas, big-bead necklaces, or wide plastic bracelets are only a few of the possibilities.

If individual novelty prizes seem inevitable, try to find those that are fairly useful, such as:

Pocket flashlights	Key rings
Ball-point pens	Automatic pencils
Coin purses	Pocket comb sets
Box of golf balls	Can of tennis balls
Memo pads	Coin banks
Miniature games	Pocket puzzles

They have the added advantage of being suitable for either men or women.

Silly prizes are the best of all, if they are suited to the person and to the game or contest. Most people would much rather win a prize that makes them laugh instead of some cheap, useless gadget they don't need. A piggy bank makes a good prize for a race like Driving the Pigs to Market; a jockey cap for races like Heigho, Silver! or Rodeo.

Couples like a prize that they can enjoy together: two tickets to a movie, chits for two sodas at the favorite teen hangout or for two meals at a local restaurant, or tickets to a ball game.

The usual blue, white and red ribbons for first, second and third places are always appropriate. Make them big and splashy, so they'll stand out. Big tin or cardboard badges sprayed gold or silver also are fun to win.

For small picnics, try to personalize the prizes or improvise them for humor. A tin cup sprayed with gilt paint makes an impressive "cup" for the winning softball team. A crown of gold-colored foil makes a Queen-of-the-Picnic out of any small girl winner. A laugh, plus the attention, plus the fun of winning, is a combination difficult to beat.

If you decide to use novelty prizes, selected for boys and girls, men and women, it's a very good idea to wrap the prizes for boys, girls, men and women in different colors of paper, or keep them in separate boxes or plastic bags, clearly labeled. A small boy will be insulted if he gets jacks or a doll for a prize. A woman may be amused but not pleased to receive a pair of suspenders instead of nylons.

The following list provides likely sources for prizes (see RESOURCES):

- Toy and game counters at the local five-and-dime. Also hardware counters, cosmetic and stationery counters.
- Same for local department stores, supermarkets, and gift shops.
- Local candy stores, bakeries.
- Mail order stores. Most of them carry all sorts of novelties that can be used for prizes.
- Special novelty stores. Consult the yellow pages of the telephone directory for local or nearby stores. Then visit or ask for a catalog. These are especially useful for holiday or special theme ideas. Such stores often are also good sources for decorations.
- Foreign gift shops, such as Japanese, Chinese, Swedish, Mexican, Italian. These often have a wide selection of pretty and inexpensive novelties that make excellent prizes.

FOOD

This book is focused mainly on picnic activities and for that reason will not contain specific picnic menus or recipes. The many varieties of cookbooks now available, plus excellent ideas in women's magazines, are all good sources for new or old recipes. Home economics departments of the local high school or state university are also good resources for information on quantity cooking.

The sandwich or covered dish picnic is all very well.

It fits into many plans, is not difficult to prepare, and can be inexpensive. Picnics whether large or small, however, need not be limited to these two familiar types. A host or hostess can establish a reputation for a special dish or type of meal that he or she has perfected. So can agency, club, church, or other group. A special kind of menu can add interest to a picnic. It can also provide an opportunity for some persons or group to shine as chefs. New outdoor cooking equipment makes experiments with menus much easier than in former days.

Every section of the nation has favorite picnic foods which are typical of that area, with their own enthusiasts. If the "makings" are available locally, there is no reason why other localities shouldn't try them. Favorites from abroad are nice changes, too.

Family or neighbor help are sufficient for small picnics. For larger and very large ones, call in the men! They'll be needed for a lot of heavy work, and they're often authorities in the preparation of certain foods. If the picnic will be very large, and/or very special, you might consider calling in a caterer or chef specializing in foreign or regional cooking. First, though, check the budget.

The following list is merely suggestive. Other ideas can be had from "old-timers," from friends and relatives living in other parts of the country, and from magazines and books. An open mind and a willingness to try something new is all that you need for a new look to your picnic.

Food Specialties

Barbecues. These are high favorites, whether using beef or chicken, whether for family or community.

Fish fries. Fish fries and hush puppies are to the South what baked beans and brown bread are to New England.

Clam bakes. New England specialty, and not nearly as difficult as they sound.

Corn roasts. Popular wherever "sweet corn" or "roasting ears" are available. Often combined with some other specialty.

Weiner roasts. All-time favorite of the youngsters and for those who like a quick-and-easy picnic.

Stews. Each kind has intense support of its enthusiasts. The old-fashioned Brunswick stew is hard to beat.

Chilis. Increasing in popularity as more and more people learn to enjoy "South of the Border" cooking.

Chicken pie dinners. A big favorite with everybody, especially hungry men. And not difficult to prepare.

Bean bakes. These are New England favorites. They may be cooked ahead of time indoors or prepared outdoors. Several different varieties.

Shish kabobs. Each person prepares his own, or the picnic chefs prepare, cook and serve. These are chunks of meat (lamb, to be authentic) plus chunks of vegetables such as onions, tomatoes, peppers. Pineapple is sometimes used, along with pork chunks. All cooked together on a long spit.

Hamburgers. Like the weiner or hot dog roasts, these are the youngsters' favorites. Easy to prepare and everybody can select his own "fixings."

Luaus. Cook-out, Hawaiian style. Food served on leaves or in wooden bowls: roast pig, pineapple in every form, poi (rice will substitute), fruit drinks.

Oriental dishes. These may include various Chinese and Japanese foods. Sukiyaki can be cooked over the outdoor fire. Other possibilities: sunflower seeds, lichee nuts, chow mein, rice, tea. Many oriental meals are now available in cans.

SHORTCUTS AND HELPFUL HINTS

- Stub ends of candles help to get a fire started.
- The soot from the fire will easily come off a pan if you rub the outside bottom and sides with shaving cream before it goes on the fire.
- A rubber band or two around a thermos or other bottle will keep it from slipping out of your hand.
- A small pocket sewed in each corner of the picnic tablecloth will keep it from blowing off in the wind. Tuck a washer or a pebble into each pocket.
- Aluminum foil crumpled up makes a good scraper for picnic dishes before they're rinsed or burned (if paper).
- You can carry charcoal easily by putting it into empty two-quart waxed, milk containers. Then just light the box to ignite the charcoal.
- Picnic cakes and cupcakes carry better if you split them and put the frosting between the slices.
- If you core apples or pears and stuff the inside with

marshmallows, the fruit won't get discolored. Use raisins, too, if your family likes them. Or cream cheese for the grown-ups. Slice the apples across when serving.

- If you put a sheet of waxed paper or foil on each paper plate as you pack them, you can serve the food on the paper or foil, gather up the "leavings" when the meal is over, and have a clean plate for salad or dessert.

- Leftover food or grease from cooking in foil can be burned off by dropping the foil into the fire for a few minutes. The foil can then be buried or placed in a trash can. Much neater and more sanitary.

- Two-tone sandwiches are interesting changes—one slice of white; the other slice of whole wheat, rye, raisin, orange, or other kind of bread.

- Melted butter soaks into the bread. To make it spread easily, it's better to use butter at room temperature, or to lighten it with half a cup of milk or mayonnaise per pound of butter.

- You can save time when making sandwiches if you lay eight or ten slices of bread in front of you, then use a spatula to spread them with the butter and any other soft filling.

- Sandwiches with fillers that are "gooey" or full of moisture should always be buttered. It helps keep the bread from getting soggy. Examples: Tomato and jelly.

- A small ice cream scoop is a good tool to use for dis-

pensing sandwich fillings like egg salad, ham or
tunafish salad.

- Sandwiches will keep fresh if you place them on
  waxed paper, cover them with waxed paper, and
  then put a damp towel or napkin under the bottom
  paper and over the top paper.

- A 2-pound pullman loaf of bread will cut into about
  35 slices, ⅜ inch thick.

- Coat hangers unwound and straightened out make
  good "toasters" for marshmallows or hot dogs. Hold
  over the fire first to make sure that any paint or
  enamel is burned off.

- A metal wheelbarrow makes a good fireholder, safe
  and easy to wheel where you want it to go. Be sure
  to put a three- or four-inch layer of sand in the bottom before you build a fire.

- Water frozen in small concentrated juice cans makes
  long-lasting cylinders of ice that you can pop into
  the thermos. They last much longer than regular ice
  cubes.

- The tailgate of a station wagon makes a fine buffet
  for an on-the-spot picnic. Use it as a worktable to
  prepare the food and then as a buffet for the sandwiches or covered dish meal.

- A pound of regular-grind coffee is about 6 cups of
  ground coffee. It will make 2½ gallons of coffee,
  about 40 cups. You don't have to have a large coffee
  urn. Just tie the coffee securely but loosely in a
  cheesecloth or muslin bag about a yard square. Drop

it into the 2½ gallons of boiling water, cover and simmer, but don't boil. Remove from the heat and keep covered for at least 10 minutes. Then swish the coffee bag up and down several times and take it out. Serve with ladle or cup.

chapter 2

INSTANT
PICNIC
ONE-GUESS
CONTESTS

One-guess contests are like parties—they may be as informal or as formal as you like. Once you decide which ones to use, all you have to do is provide whatever is needed and, in some cases, find the correct answer ahead of time.

These contests will help you over two shaky spots in any picnic, the Start-Off and the End-Up. Suppose you have asked twenty friends for a back yard picnic. They dribble in with their children. You need something to pull them together in a common interest. That watermelon you plan to serve for dessert is the answer. How much does it weigh in pounds and ounces? And no fair touching!

Or suppose you are on the program committee for the annual Fourth of July Community Picnic. A good Start-Off guessing contest will break the ice and get folks talking to each other. It also lures them to a central gathering place, and that makes the announcing and handling of the picnic events much easier.

Sometime later, when it's almost time for the picnic to

end, families may begin to drift away. That's when some good End-Ups will hold them and provide final entertainment. Ending with a bang is much more exciting than fizzling out.

START-OFFS

Some of these contests can be completed at once. Others can be carried over, with the winner being announced toward the end of the picnic. In case of the latter, they become part of the End-Up. Often the size of the group is a determining factor.

1. CLOCK WATCHER

You'll need: The biggest, noisiest alarm clock you can find. Perhaps a dishpan, to amplify the sound. Small slips of paper for each guess. A bag or bucket to hold the guesses. A judge to go over the guesses and find the winner and runner-up.

What to do: Announce that the alarm will go off sometime during the picnic. Hand out the slips of paper. Ask each person to make a guess at the exact hour and minute of the alarm. Appoint a judge to select the winner and runner-up. Set the alarm clock face down or where its face is hidden.

Prize: The alarm clock. Toy wrist watch. Time card with gold star.

Be careful: Make sure the clock goes off properly. Make a note of the time set and give it to the judge.

2. KORN KERNELS

You'll need: An ear of corn, the shucks and silk drawn back to show the kernels. An official Kernel Kounter. Bag or box for guesses.

What to do: Announce the contest. Give out paper slips. Collect the guesses. Appoint or ask for a Korn Kounter to find the korrect kount, determine winner and runner-up.

Prize: Decorative corn cluster for front door. A dozen "roasting ears." A bag of candy corn.

Be careful: Make sure no one touches the ear of corn, or gets too close. Provide the Korn Kounter with a darning needle, ice pick, or other sharp object. If he punctures each kernel, his counting will be easier.

3. HAM HOIST

You'll need: A ham, chicken, lobster, watermelon or other heavy object. Paper slips for weight guessing. A scale. Official hoister.

What to do: Place the object in plain sight or hang up out of reach. Announce the contest. Give out and collect the guesses. Appoint a hoister to weigh the object. Announce the person with the nearest correct guess in pounds and ounces.

Prizes: The ham, chicken, lobster, watermelon or other object being guessed.

4. STAND STILL

You'll need: Some very inconspicuous object marking a special place in the picnic area selected ahead of time—

such as a stake driven all the way into the ground, a small white mark, a special tree. A yardstick, just in case. A whistle.

What to do: Announce that there is a lucky or magic spot somewhere in the area. Ask everyone to mill around until the whistle blows, then to stand stock still. Go out and find the person nearest the lucky spot, measuring if necessary.

Prize: A good luck charm. A lucky coin. A gold paper crown (for children).

Be careful: Make sure the marker is something that can't be picked up, pushed away, or destroyed by tramping feet.

5. Wig Wag

You'll need: A wig, real or make-believe (make-believe, out of rope, yarn or a mop, will be easier to use). Paper slips for guessing. An official Wig Wag to count the hairs (or strings) of the wig.

What to do: Display the wig, on somebody if possible. Announce the contest. Give out paper slips and collect the guesses. Appoint someone (a man for a woman's wig, a woman for a man's toupee) as the Wig Wag.

Prize: The wig or toupee. Artificial eyelashes. Artificial beard or mustache. Doll wig (for little girls). Ticket for a shampoo and set (for women).

Be careful: Real wigs and hair pieces are expensive. Use imitation, nylon, or plain fake. The contest will be just as amusing.

6. Petal Puller

You'll need: A large many-petaled flower, such as a rose, chrysanthemum, zinnia, sunflower, perhaps from your own garden.

What to do: Show the flower. Appoint a tally keeper. Ask for guesses as to the number of petals. Instruct the tally keeper to list the name and guess of each person. Then one by one, pull off the petals dramatically and count them out loud (It's fun if everyone joins in and chants "One, two," etc.). When the poor flower is petal-less, ask the tally keeper to announce the person whose guess was the nearest to the correct answer.

Prize: A bouquet from your garden. A flower lei. An outsize plastic rose. A package of flower seeds.

Variation: Use this counting technique for other guessing contests. The number of beans in a glass or gallon jug. The number of nails in a keg. The number of apples in a bushel basket. The number of berries in a quart basket.

7. Fine Print

You'll need: A front page, an editorial, or a column from the newspaper. The correct answer to the number of words if the contest is a quickee.

What to do: Announce the contest. Display the news page. Give out and collect paper slips for guesses. Appoint an official reader to count the words of the chosen page or section (a, an, the, I, me, all count) and announce the correct total. Announce the winner of the guess nearest to the correct answer.

Prize: A magnifying glass. A subscription to the local newspaper. A storybook (for children).

Be careful: The reader will find it helpful to dab each word with a red pencil. Helps him keep the place—and count!

8. MYSTERY MAN AND MRS. X

You'll need: A dime-store ring or special coin, or other special token for Mystery Man and Mrs. X to carry.

What to do: Ahead of time, select Mystery Man and Mrs. (or Miss) X and swear them to secrecy. Give each the special token. On picnic day announce the contest and tell the folks that Mrs. X and Mystery Man are in the group.

Rules: People must ask any man or woman if he or she is Mr. Mystery Man or Mrs. X. Mystery Man and Mrs. X will answer NO to each person who questions them, but the *tenth* (or other) person who asks the question gets the token. He or she turns it in to the emcee and gets a special prize.

Prize: This can be the very best prize of the picnic or a just-for-fun prize. Jigsaw puzzle. Eye mask. Box of candy. Mirror. Detective story.

END-UPS

These are sometimes the results of the Start-Offs, but they don't have to be. Often they are personalized guessing contests, designed to point out specific people, compliment or tease them—all in a good-natured way. They are really the happy endings for picnics.

9. Who Is, Who Has?

You'll need: A microphone or cheerleader's horn. Voices don't carry well outdoors.

What to do: Appoint several recorders. Ask for nominations. Ask for candidates. Get each recorded. Award prizes to winners.

Questions to ask:
- The oldest person here
- The youngest
- The tallest
- The youngest grandmother
- Who traveled farthest to come
- Who has the most girls
- Who has the most boys
- The smallest foot (women)
- The youngest mother
- The largest foot (men)
- The fanciest hairdo
- The longest last name
- The shortest last name
- Has lived longest in the community
- Birth date nearest the picnic date
- The oldest car
- Married the longest time
- Married the shortest time
- The longest hair (girls and women)
- The longest beard

The most freckles (girl)
The most freckles (boy)

Prizes: Throw-outs are fun. These can be simple, bright, gay things like leis for the women. Wide-brimmed hats for men. Balloons. Apples. Oranges. Lollipops. Ticket to movie. Good luck charm. Cowboy neckerchiefs. Bright plastic bracelets or beads. Bright shopping bags. Roses. Pennants. Distribute them generously. Folks like souvenirs and take-homes.

INSTANT

SCRAMBLES

chapter 3

PICNIC

Scrambles are simple contests with almost no rules. They are strictly each-for-himself contests. They give the Under-Sixes a part in the picnic program that they can understand and enjoy.

Preschoolers have not yet learned how to play together as a group. They are not old enough to understand rules, taking turns, playing fair, or teamwork. They *are* old enough to like to be with other children and to get adult attention. They also like prizes, although they don't understand the idea of rewards for winning a game.

Scrambles are based on the simple child reaction, "I see it. I want it." They are giveaways, where every child gets some sort of simple prize: a balloon, a penny, lollipops, a flag, an Easter egg, marbles.

Grown-ups enjoy them almost as much as the youngsters. After all, what is more fun than seeing the satisfied expression on the face of a small girl as she finds a lollipop, or the concentration of a little boy as he tries to grab several pieces of candy in his small hands? Adult enthusiasm can be too great and can over-stimulate the youngsters. Keep the scrambles informal, relaxed, keyed down. Try to minimize the proud-parent act.

Make sure, too, that every child gets a token award, even if he has burst into tears and refused to play. He's too young to understand losing. Keep the scrambles friendly, with someone nearby to help, encourage, or console.

10. LOLLIPOP SCRAMBLE

You'll need: An open area—the more children, the larger the area. Good supply of lollipops, enough for several per child. Somebody to line the children up behind a starting line. Somebody to stick the lollipops about a foot apart into the ground in a long line about 30 feet from the children. A whistle or other starting device.

What to do: See that the children are selected by ages and by height. Run the scramble, if need be, several times to make sure that a big five-year-old boy isn't pitted against a dainty three-year-old girl. Line the youngsters up behind the starting lines. Tell them that when the whistle blows, they are to run out, pick up the lollipops, and come back to the starting line. Ask parents to stay out of playing area, but be on hand for the child's return.

Variations: Use small flags for patriotic day picnics. Easter eggs for spring picnics.

Be careful: Save some lollipops for a rerun for any youngsters who wandered off or were too late to get any. Warn youngsters not to run with lollipops in mouths. See that the lollipops or other awards in this kind of scramble are well scattered to avoid collisions.

11. CANDY SHOWER (MEXICAN PIÑATA)

You'll need: A homemade or purchased paper or papier-mâché container (The real Mexican ones come in all sorts of shapes—cowboys, fish, birds, clowns, butterflies, donkeys, all gaily painted. Big, brown-paper grocery bags, dressed up with poster paints, make good substitutes.). Wrapped candies and small novelty gifts to fill the bag. A rope to hang it over the limb of a tree or other place where it can dangle. Cane or stick for hitting it. Blindfold for the hitter.

What to do: Ahead of time make, prepare or purchase the piñata. Fill it with goodies. Select its hanging place. Select a man or husky teen-ager to hold the rope and possibly to help break the piñata. At picnic time, hang the piñata up. Explain to the children that they should scramble for the goodies that will fall out when the piñata breaks. Line them up so that each can have a whack at it with the cane. Blindfold each child when his turn comes up. Signal the rope-holder to raise and lower the piñata at times to keep the suspense high.

Variations: Parents can take turns being blindfolded, turned around several times, then given the cane to whack the piñata, leaving the children ready for action. Make the piñata from several layers of bright tissue paper if very young children will try to hit it, for easier breaking and faster scrambling. Fill the bag with unshelled peanuts for a peanut scramble.

Be careful: You have no idea how *tough* brown paper, or a cardboard box, or a real papier-mâché piñata can be! Keep the youngsters well away from the cane as well as the rope-handler. Be ready to console some tenderhearted boy or girl who can't bear to see the piñata cowboy, or donkey, or bird beaten by that awful cane! Hold out some of the goodies—there'll be some child too excited or startled to get his share.

12. Toe Holds

You'll need: An open area, hopefully grassy. A supply of wrapped hard candies or pretty glass marbles. A small brown paper bag for each child. Blindfolds for each child. Whistle or other starting and stopping device.

What to do: Line the youngsters up barefooted, around the edges of the play area (a 30-foot square is a good size). Ask parents or helpers to blindfold each child. Give each child a small paper bag. Explain that the area is full of treasures but they must be located by the feet! At the signal, everyone must start to feel around with his bare feet, pick up everything he finds, put it in his bag, and stop hunting when the whistle blows again.

Prizes: The bag of candies or marbles found. Extra prize for the largest number found. Extra prize for any special colored candy wrapper or outsize marble.

Be careful: Make sure the playing area is free from glass or other objects that might hurt bare feet. For children frightened by blindfolds, use brown paper bag over the head to permit a glimpse of the ground. Hold out a supply of the treasure for the child who loses his or doesn't find any. Be prepared to run a second scramble if most of the candies or marbles aren't found the first time. Make sure everybody gets his shoes and socks back on (better have parents hold them). Encourage "scavenging" for any unfound treasure when the hunt is over.

13. SAND CENTS (PENNY SCRAMBLE)

You'll need: A fenced or walled-in sandpile or a clearly marked beach or other sand area. A number of bright, new pennies (the more children, the larger the sand area and the more pennies).

What to do: Ahead of time, count the pennies so you'll know when all have been found. Hide them in the sand area. Explain that finders are keepers. Line youngsters up around the sand area. Explain that they can start digging when the whistle blows, but must stop for a penny count when the whistle blows again. Every now and then, blow whistle for a count to see how many pennies are left. Finally announce that only one (or two or three) pennies are left. Offer a special prize for the finder of that Last Red Cent.

Variations: If sand area is limited, such as a sandbox, run several scrambles. Five children at a time are as many as the average home sandbox can hold for this scramble. Use foil-covered candy coins instead of pennies.

Prize: The pennies found. Extra prize for the most or the last three found might be a sand bucket set. A bright new dime.

Be careful: Make sure the sand area has no broken glass or other litter. Allow no spoons, spades or other tools. Absolutely no sand throwing (if it can't be prevented, water the sand well). Hold out some of the pennies, real or fake, for the child who doesn't find any or for a rerun if several miss out.

14. NEEDLE IN THE HAYSTACK

You'll need: A fenced-in, level area waist high with hay or straw (Snow fences will make adequate barriers. Buckwheat husks, peat moss, sawdust or other soft but bulky material can substitute for hay, but they lack the resistance that hay gives.). Lots of small, gay but inexpensive articles, such as balls, whistles, balloons, lollipops, wrapped hard candies, toys, miniature toys and dolls.

What to do: Prepare the playing area ahead of time. Count and hide the treasures all through it. Line the youngsters up around the outer edge of the playing area. Explain that when the whistle blows, the hunt is on; and when it blows again, everyone must stop and show what he has found. Station a few teen-agers or parent helpers around, to give encouragement or solace. Keep count of the number and stop the hunt when you know all the treasures have been found.

Prizes: What they find they may keep.

Variations: Play in short time periods. Require each child to leave when he has found a prize.

Be careful: Some children get very frustrated by the hay. See that they either are helped to find a prize, or are gently

taken from the hunt and given a prize outside. If one or two
children find the prizes too rapidly, call a time limit or
allow only one prize each. Discourage hay tossing—it fright-
ens some children. Look out for flying feet, elbows and
knees. Any child sneezing or wheezing should be taken out
of the hay at once. Hold out a supply of the treasures for
reruns or for consolation for those who couldn't find anything. Have parents or teen-age helpers ready to brush off
the youngsters after the scramble. Make arrangements for
the disposal of the hay after the picnic.

15. Balloon Catch

You'll need: A supply of blown-up balloons. One balloon with a small x or other special mark on it. A level,
smooth or grassy area about 30 feet long. A whistle for a
starter.

What to do: Line the youngsters up behind a starting
line. Place the inflated balloons side by side on a line about
30 feet away from the starting line. Explain that at the signal each child must race up to the line and then bring the
balloon back to the starting line. Explain that one balloon is
X-tra Special, and whoever gets it gets an X-tra prize.

Prizes: The balloon. Something X-tra, such as a storybook, paint set, doll, cowboy hat.

Variations: The youngsters must kick the balloons back
to the starting line (best for those seven, eight and nine
years old). Youngsters try to get as many balloons as possible.

Be careful: Make sure the youngsters are evenly matched in age or size. Hold back extra balloons to replace those that get broken. Keep extras for children who fail to bring a balloon back.

INSTANT

chapter 4

PICNIC CONTESTS

What would a picnic be without contests for the small-fry, the boys, the girls, the grown-ups? Without races and relays? It just wouldn't be a picnic!

You'll find that contests and races are easier to manage, give each player more of a fair chance, and are usually more physically suitable if you'll divide the youngsters into quite small age groupings. This will vary a bit, depending on the number of youngsters involved. If it is reasonable, groupings of two- or three-year intervals will keep the skill levels more equal. For example, seven- and eight-year-olds are more nearly equal than seven-to-tens.

When the number of youngsters is too small to warrant such small groupings, you can always "handicap" the older youngsters. Their starting line (or finish line) might be so placed that they must race a bit farther.

It is also wise to separate by sex youngsters over six years old. Here again, when the number of children does not permit it, the boys can be given handicaps. Children under six

18. Big Push

You'll need: A balloon for each player (different colors, if possible). A starting line. A finish line about 30 feet away. Judges to pick the winners.

What to do: Line up the players behind the starting line, balloon on line in front of each. At signal, each player bats his balloon along the ground to the finish line. Judges select the first three to cover the line.

Prizes: A big balloon. Lollipop. Bubble gum. Small toy.

Variations: Players must fan the balloon with a fan made of pleated paper (but not touch the balloon). Players must balance the balloon on the palm of one hand and carry it over the finish line. Players must push the balloon over the finish line by using a stick or cane. Players must kick the balloon over the finish line.

Be careful: When using this race for young children, shorten the distance. Have extra balloons on hand to replace any that break. If using canes, keep contestants well separated.

19. Bow Wow

You'll need: A starting line. Finish line about 30 feet away. Judges for winners.

What to do: Line the players up behind the starting line, each down on all fours, like a dog. At signal, each doggie must run to the finish line, barking loudly all the way.

Prizes: Toy dog. Dog collar. Dog tag.

Variations: Same race, but for cats—each kitten must meow all the way. Same for donkeys—when the donkey gets to the finish line, he must kick up his heels, yell "Hee Haw!" and run back to the starting line.

Be careful. Make sure the playing area is clear of all glass or other litter.

20. KICK OFF

You'll need: A bean bag or substitute (balloon, stick, waxed milk container or other object that won't roll too well) for each player. Starting line. Finish line. Judges to pick winners.

What to do: Line up the players behind the starting line. Each player gets into crab position, on hands and feet, but face up. At signal, each walks crab fashion, sideways, kicking the bean bag toward the finish line. First to get the bean bag over is the winner.

Prize: Can of crabmeat. Sign, "I am a crab." Candy bar. Balloon.

Be careful: Make sure the playing area is clear of all glass or other litter.

21. TIE UP

You'll need: For each player, a package of Life Savers or other candy-with-a-hole-in-the-middle. A piece of string about a yard long. Judge to pick the winner.

What to do: Players stand anywhere in playing area. Each must unwrap the candy, thread one of the candies onto the string, tie it in place, add the second candy, tie it, and so on, until each of the candies in the package has been strung on and tied to the string. First to finish must take the string to the judge.

Prizes: Box of candy. Bead necklace. Package of shoe-strings.

Be careful: Make sure that the winning string has the correct number of candies on it.

22. Sore Toe Race

You'll need: A starting line. A finish line about 50 feet away. Judge to pick the winner.

What to do: Line the players up behind the starting line. Each must extend either leg in front of him as straight as possible and grasp the toes with one hand. In that position, the player must hop to the finish line. The other hand cannot be used to help hold the extended foot.

Prizes: Roll of bandages. Band aids. Candy corn. Toy car. Toy doctor set. Candy bar. Bubble gum.

23. Shuffle Off

You'll need: Two potatoes for each player. A starting line. A finish line. Judge to pick the winner.

What to do: Line up the players behind the starting line. Place a potato (or substitute, such as a block of wood) on each foot of each player. At signal, each must "shuffle off" to the finish line. If a potato falls off, it must be replaced before moving on. First to reach finish line wins.

Prizes: Doll's shoes. Jazz record. Bag of potato chips.

Be careful: Select potatoes that are not too round.

24. FLYING SAUCERS

You'll need: A level, smooth, playing area with spectators roped off. A dish pan (metal or plastic) for each contestant. A target line about 30 feet away from the starting line. Judges with yardsticks to measure the throws.

What to do: Line up the players along the starting line. Give each a dish pan. At signal, each spins his dish pan along the ground toward the target line, trying to get the pan as close to the line as possible. When all players have had their turns, measure the distances of those pans closest to the line. Any pan touching the line scores 5 points; if the pan does not touch the line, the one closest to the line scores 3 points. Play a round of three (each player gets three turns), and give prizes to players with the two highest scores.

Prizes: Toy bowling ball. The dish pan. Blue, red or white ribbon.

Variations: Use foil or tin pie plates instead of dish pans. Players form two teams instead of playing separately. Play with husband and wife contestants. Men versus women.

Be careful: Make sure spectators stay out of the target area. A spinning dish pan can give quite a blow to the shins! Post guards to fend off any wild "shots."

25. BOAT RACE

You'll need: A bamboo or other pole about 6 feet long (the local department store might have one in its rug or rug-wrapping department). An open area with a starting line and some object such as a tree, chair, or stake at the end of the rowing course, about 25 yards away. Crews of five players for each "racing shell," plus a coxswain to steer the boat. A starter. Judges for first, second and third winners.

What to do: Line up the "crews," who straddle the pole, backs to the course. The coxswain straddles the pole, facing forward. At the signal, each "crew" races toward the stake. The coxswain directs them around it and back to the finish line. Separate judges decide first, second and third places.

Prizes: Model boat. Pennant. Key chain. Wallet. Blue, white and red ribbons.

Be careful: This race is best for the strong and healthy. Make the distance shorter for adults or the lower-age teens. Good for husky teen-age boys.

26. SHOE FLY

You'll need: A starting line. Judge to mark and measure the distance.

What to do: Line up the players behind the starting line. Each player removes one shoe and dangles it loosely on the toes. On signal, each kicks that foot out, trying to toss the shoe as far as possible. Judge marks the farthest, measuring in case of doubt.

Prizes: A gilded horseshoe. Horseshoe charm. Doll shoes. Horseshoe game set.

Be careful: Make sure the spectators are out of range. Ask for volunteers for races of this type (not everyone wants to take off a shoe).

27. SACK RACE

You'll need: A burlap sack for each player. A starting line. A finish line about 30 feet away (shorter for young children, farther for older ones). Judge to pick first three winners.

What to do: Line up the players back of the starting line—each inside a burlap bag, holding it up around him with his hands. At signal, players run (or try to) to finish line. Judge picks first, second and third winner, or the winning boy and girl.

Prizes: Box of Cracker Jack. Bubble gum. Candy bars. Outsize sunglasses. Bag of marbles. Jacks.

Variations: If large bags are available, try putting two children in each bag (but shorten the distance). Run in heats—four or five youngsters race, then another group, etc., and finally all the winners try for the Big Win.

Be careful: Sack races always have lots of spills. Be ready to comfort. Be ready to treat skinned knees or elbows.

28. HEAVY, HEAVY HANGS OVER YOUR HEAD

You'll need: A paper cup or container filled two-thirds full of water for each player. Starting line. Finish line about 30 feet away. Judge to pick the winner.

What to do: Line up the players behind the starting line. Give each a cup or paper container of water to place on head. At signal each tries to be first to get to the finish line without dropping the cup.

Prizes: Cold soft drink. Ticket for a soda at the local drugstore. Head scarf. Plastic rain hat.

Variations: Use any object instead of paper cup—an apple, block of wood. Try a pie pan with several peanuts on it.

Be careful: Get volunteers for this water race. Girls and women often don't want to get their hair wet; offer them plastic head coverings. Provide paper towels for mop up. If apples or other substitute items fall, they must be picked up and replaced before the player may continue.

29. HOOPLA!

You'll need: Eleven barrel hoops. Twenty-two men or strong boys to hold those hoops. A starting line. A finish line 60 to 75 feet away. Judge on the finish line.

What to do: Line up the hoops in hourglass fashion— three in the first line, two in the second, one in the center of the area, then two behind, then three. Each of these lines of hoops should be about 15 feet apart. The men or boys hold each hoop steady and upright, but touching the ground. Line up six players back of the starting line. At the signal, each must run through any *one* of the first three hoops and *either* of the next two, all players must go through the single center hoop, then through either of the next two, and through any one of the last three hoops. First player to dash over the finish line wins.

Prizes: Decorated hoop. Jacks. Top. Bag of marbles. Candy bar. Miniature car.

Variations: Run in heats, with a final race for winners. Vary the number of hoops. Put some of the hoops in tunnel formation.

Be careful: The boys or men must hold those hoops firmly and keep them steady.

30. SIAMESE TWINS

You'll need: A starting line. A finish line about 50 feet away. Judges to pick the winners.

What to do: Line the "twins" up behind the starting line—they stand back to back, elbows hooked. On signal, they run (one forward, one backward) to the finish line. Without turning around, they race back to the starting line (the player who went out backwards comes back facing the line). If they fall, they must get up and continue in same position. First twins to cross the starting line win.

Prizes: Toy handcuffs. Tickets for local movie. Chit for two chocolate sodas.

Be careful: Warn players about falling. The player running forward should keep feet close together. Player going backward should keep feet wide apart.

31. BALL-ON-BOTTLE RELAY

You'll need: A level, smooth area about 100 feet long. Six pop bottles and six golf balls for each team. Two teams of about five or six players each. A starting line. Judge to pick the winner.

What to do: Ahead of time, stand three pop bottles in path of each team, about 50 feet from the starting line. Balance a golf ball on the top of each. Fifty feet from these pop bottles, set up three more for each team (but without the golf balls). On signal, the first player on each team runs to the first set of bottles, takes off the golf balls, runs to the second set of bottles and puts a golf ball on each, then races back to touch player number 2 of his team. Player number 2 runs to the *last* set of bottles, takes the balls, and places them on the first set of bottles, then runs back and touches player number 3. And so on until the last player of one team has crossed the starting line before the other team has finished.

Prizes: A bottle of ice-cold pop for each player. Golf balls. Toy golf club.

Variations: Use same rules, but different objects. For example, two pans per team, one pan holding three potatoes.

Be careful: If a bottle is knocked over or a golf ball dropped, it must be replaced properly before the runner can go on. Reduce distances for younger children or to suit the picnic area.

32. BANANA BEAT

You'll need: Twelve players. Twelve bananas. Judges to decide the winner. (Fewer or more players can be used. This race is fun with only two contestants.)

What to do: Divide players into three relay teams, four players on each. Teams line up behind their captains. Each player must put his left hand behind his back and keep it there. Place a banana in the right hand of player number 1 (the captain) on each team. At the signal, each captain must peel the banana with his teeth, then eat it as quickly as possible, holding it with the right hand. When he has finished eating it, he must whistle loud enough for the judges to hear. At that moment, the judge gives player number 2 a banana. He follows the same procedure, peeling and eating the banana as fast as possible. And so on until each person or team has whistled. Team finishing first wins.

Prizes: Bunch of bananas. Bag of banana candy. Chit for banana sundaes at the local drugstore. Banner saying TOP BANANA.

Be careful: It is a good plan never to use an eating contest with very small children who might choke. Make sure the banana skins are picked up.

33. Kangaroo Race

You'll need: A starting line. A finish line about 30 feet away. A balloon for each player. A judge to pick the winners.

What to do: Line the players up behind the starting line. Each holds a balloon between his knees. At the signal, they all hop like kangaroos to the finish line. Balloons must not be broken or dropped. First over the line wins.

Prizes: Toy animal. Candy bar. Soda pop.

Variations: Use an orange instead of balloon. Or a soft rubber ball.

Be careful: Eliminate any player who drops or breaks the balloon. Use contest with care—it is more strenuous than it seems. Oranges sometimes squish, so use them only when knees are bare or stains don't matter.

34. CHEF BASTING

You'll need: Ten or 15 "chefs." A tall paper bag and a folded newspaper "swatter" for each chef. A large level circle about 20 feet in diameter.

What to do: Each "chef" puts on his tall chef's hat. At the signal each chef tries to knock the hats off other chefs, while preserving his own. Players must leave the area when they lose their hats. Last chef left in the ring is the winner.

Prizes: A chef's hat. Man's apron. Potholder. Bag of charcoal.

Be careful: Be sure no one keeps eyeglasses on. Keep spectators out of swatting range. Make circle large enough to permit some fancy footwork.

35. ROOSTER FIGHT

You'll need: A six-foot circle for each pair of young "cocks." Two broomsticks.

What to do: Place two contestants in each circle. Each player most hold a broomstick under his knees, hands under the stick and grasped together in front. At signal, each tries to push the other out of the circle.

Prizes: Bag of candy corn. Blue ribbon. Gold star. Toy alarm clock.

Variations: Winner challenges new "cock" until all contestants have had a try. Run cock fights in several circles, with winners in each fighting other winners until final winning Rooster is left undefeated. Players grasp their ankles instead of the sticks.

Be careful: This is fairly rough. Make sure the contestants are well matched in age and weight. Keep spectators back, well outside the circles.

36. RODEO

You'll need: Four "cowboys." Four cardboard or wooden boxes. Four broomsticks. Four sharpened sticks. Twelve potatoes. Starting line. Judges to pick winner.

What to do: Place three potatoes in a row in front of each player, and about 30 feet away. Line up players behind starting line, giving each a broomstick to straddle. Give each a spear (sharpened stick). At signal each cowboy races out to his line of potatoes to spear one potato, races with it on his spear back to the starting line and puts it in his box, and so on until one player gets all of his potatoes back in his box before the others.

Prizes: Cowboy bandannas. Lariat. Cowboy hat.

Variations: Play as a relay. Each player runs out, spears one potato, brings it back to the box, hands spear to player number 2, etc. Play as a substitute for the usual potato race by providing enough equipment for more players at a time.

Or run in heats, with finalists competing for the Grand
Rodeo.

Be careful: Collect all the spears as soon as race is over.
Remove brooms, boxes and potatoes. For younger children
use spoons instead of spears.

37. STRETCH IT!

You will need: Relay teams of around five players each.
For each team, an elastic band made by sewing together the
ends of an 18-inch length of ¼-inch elastic. A judge to
decide the winning team.

What to do: Line teams up behind captains (player number 1 on each team). Give each captain one of the elastic
bands. At signal the captain on each team must pull it over
his head, down around his body and step out of it. He then
passes it to player number 2 who *steps into* it, pulls it *up*
his body and over his head. He passes it to player number 3
who puts the band over his head, down his body and steps
out of it. And so on, alternating the action. First team to
finish the "stretch" wins.

Prizes: Pair of suspenders. Pair of sleeve garters. Tape
measure.

Variations: Use a barrel hoop instead of the elastic. Have
each player use the same method (stepping into or pulling
over head) instead of alternating them.

Be careful: Unless girls or women are in slacks, use only
the over-the-head action for either hoop or elastic. If teens
are mixed, alternate men and women so that the men step

into the elastic or hoop and the women pull it over their heads.

38. BEAN PASS

You'll need: Relay teams of about five players each. A paper cup and soda straw for each player. Five beans for each team. A judge.

What to do: Line up the teams behind their captains (player number 1). Give each player a paper cup and a soda straw. At signal, player number 1 on each team transfers the five beans, one by one, from his cup into the cup of player number 2, doing this by sucking into his straw so that the bean will be held at the end of the straw. Player number 2 passes the beans along to player number 3 by using the same method. When the five beans have been transferred into the cup of the last player on the team, he must run with his cup to the judge. First player to show his beans wins.

Prizes: Can of baked beans. Balloon. Rattle or maraca. Nut candy bar.

Be careful: Make sure the beans are too big to be sucked up into the straw.

39. STEP ON IT

You'll need: Definite playing area, preferably a circle about 15 feet in diameter. Eight players per circle. Balloon on a yard of string.

What to do: Fasten a balloon to the left ankle of each player, leaving the balloon plenty of leeway (about two

feet of the string). Players move around inside the circle but cannot step out of it. Each tries to step on other players' balloons, using the right foot, while protecting his own balloon. When a player's balloon bursts, he must leave the circle. Last player with balloon intact is the winner.

Prizes: An outsize balloon. Toy spurs.

Be careful: This is fun to watch but it's rough. Better limit it to boys or men. Have band aids handy for scraped ankles.

40. Wash-Day Relay

You'll need: Relay teams of five or six players each. A large towel and two clothespins for each team. A starting line. A clothes line stretched (or held) about 30 feet away. Judge to select winning team.

What to do: Give a towel and two clothespins to the captain (player number 1) of each team. At signal each captain must run to the clothes line and hang the towel to it with the two clothespins. He runs back and touches player number 2. Player number 2 runs back to the line, unpins the towel and brings it and the clothespins back to player number 3. And so on, until all the players of one team are back in place.

Prizes: Bag of clothespins. Jump rope. Box of soap flakes. Doll's clothespins. Candy bars.

Variations: For individual contest, provide several items to be pinned up—such as blue jeans, shirt, pair of socks. Make it harder and funnier by making a rule that the players must keep their right or left hands behind them (yes, teeth are allowed!).

Be careful: If the clothes line is held by two people, it should be kept taut. If towel and clothes line are borrowed, be sure to return them.

INSTAN

PICNIC
COUPLE
CONTESTS

chapter 5

Sometimes couples are left out of picnic fun, or are given the role of spectators only. The young and the very active play a big part in picnic activities, but don't forget the parents, the grandparents, the young married couples, the going-steadies. While Junior wants to show off his racing skill and Sissie strives for her blue ribbon, there are many people who feel uneasy or unhappy when separated from their partners.

Many twosomes just don't want to be broken down into onesomes, or combined into teams with other people. They enjoy being together. They will take part in and thoroughly enjoy any activities that keep them together as a couple, with or against other couples.

And that's great—because many of the very best picnic activities are *couple* activities. Many are exciting. Most of them are amusing. Some in this chapter might very well fit into Chapter 6, the laugh-makers. Don't hesitate to change any of the contests in Chapter 4 into couple contests, if they'll work out best for you.

It's usually best to ask for volunteers. But when you know the people, call them out by name. And it's a very good idea to get several couples into the act, so that one couple doesn't feel too conspicuous. Nobody likes to be the goat—unless there are lots of goats!

Keep couple contests moving. The more momentum, the less hanging back you'll encounter. Give spectators plenty of room to watch. Try to keep the couples moving from spectators to participants, so that everyone gets involved.

One of the very nicest things about couple contests is that it brings couples together. Two people come to the picnic knowing each other but not many others. When they leave, they have met other couples and new friendships have been born. That's why people are the most important element in picnics.

41. DOUBLE TAKE ✗

You'll need: Any number of couples. A tin cup, tablespoon, mirror, and can of peanuts for each couple. Spectator space, because everyone will try to see. A judge assigned to each couple. A timekeeper.

What to do: One person sits or stands, holding the tin cup on his head with his left hand and the tablespoon in his right hand. His partner holds the can of peanuts in one hand and a small mirror in the other. The one with the spoon must dip into the can of peanuts and then try to drop the peanuts into the tin cup on his head *while looking into the mirror*. Call time in two minutes. Judges count the peanuts in the cup. Couple with the most peanuts in the cup wins.

Prizes: The rest of the peanuts. Can of nuts. Nut candy bar.

Variations: Count the peanuts that fell around each couple; couple with the fewest number wins. Play again, reversing the couple (woman holds cup and spoon, man holds peanut supply and mirror).

Be careful: Women with elaborate hairdos won't want to spoil them. Collect all equipment and litter.

42. MARSHMALLOW MADNESS

You'll need: One or more couples. A marshmallow for each player. Blindfolds for each person. A circle or platform so that everybody can see.

What to do: Place the couples so that each person faces his partner about arm's length away. Blindfold each. Give each a marshmallow. At signal each tries to feed the marshmallow to his partner. First couple to succeed in feeding each other wins.

Prizes: Mirror for the girl, hand towel for the man. Box of marshmallows. Toasting forks. Box of charcoal briquets.

Variations: If you know the players well, and are sure they'll take it as a joke, substitute marshmallows that have been smoked and are sooty. Instead of white on the face, the dabs will be black (small boys like this!) Any food that is harmlessly messy, such as ice cream cones for children, bananas (see Activity 46).

Be careful: Don't use sooty marshmallows (except with children, who seldom mind things like that) unless you know the couple. Women and older girls won't like their makeup being spoiled. Very shy or self-conscious people might not like it, either. Men and boys don't mind. Provide a wet towel for cleanup.

43. Button, Button

You'll need: A needle, a length of thread and a button for each couple. An inspector to pick the fastest and best button sewer.

What to do: Give each man a needle, and line the men up about 15 feet from the women. Give each woman a length of thread and a button (thimbles optional!). At signal, each woman runs to her partner. He holds the needle up. She must thread it without touching it and then sew the button on his coat or sleeve. First to finish must run to the inspector for approval.

Prizes: Sewing kit. Outsize thimble.

Variations: Award separate prize for neatness if race seems too easy. Substitute a clothes patch for the button.

Be careful: Collect the needles when the race is over—they're dangerous for bare feet. Try to get women with good vision so they won't have trouble threading the needles.

44. Queen Elizabeth's Race

You'll need: A smooth, level playing area. Two pieces of cardboard or burlap for each couple (the cardboards that laundries use in folding men's shirts are a good size). A starting line. A finish line about 50 or 60 feet away. A starter. Judges to select the three fastest couples.

What to do: Line up the couples behind the starting line. The Sir Walter Raleighs hold the two pieces of cardboard. On signal each man lays one of the cardboards on the ground, and each woman puts one of her feet on it. The man then lays the other cardboard, the woman steps on it, and so on to the finish line. If a woman steps on the ground, she and her partner must leave the race.

Prizes: Blue, white and red ribbons. Paperback book of etiquette. Doll or child's play cape.

Be careful: This race is hard on the men's backs and the women's balance. Use with young adults. Require older men to stay on their knees (it'll be easier than bending each time).

45. WEDDING RING RACE

You'll need: A Life Saver (or other candy with a hole through it) for each woman. A wooden or plastic toothpick for each man. A starting line. A goal line. A starter. Judges to select the three winning couples.

What to do: Line up the women on the starting line. Each woman holds the candy in her lips. Men line up on goal line, facing partners, and holding the toothpicks in their mouths. At signal each woman runs to her partner, tries to slip the candy onto the toothpick without using her hands and without the man using his hands. When the ring is on the toothpick, the couple join hands and run back to the starting line. The ring must not fall from the toothpick. Judges select the first three couples to get back.

Prizes: Brass curtain ring. Blue, white and red ribbons. Package of mints. Package of colored plastic toothpicks.

Be careful: Use this type of contest with older teen-agers and adults. For older adults, modify the distance and require walking.

46. BANANA BASH

You'll need: A ripe banana and a blindfold for each couple. Roped-off open area for the players. A starter. Judges to pick first, second and third winners.

What to do: Call up the couples. Give each person a banana. Scatter the couples around so that spectators can see them all. Blindfold each person. At signal each couple starts to feed the banana to each other. Judges pick first three couples to finish. Award a special prize to the couple with the neatest faces, the messiest faces.

Prizes: Blue, white and red ribbons. Dozen bananas. Chit for banana split at local drugstore or malt shop. Tickets to movie.

Variations: Use well-cooked hot dog, complete with roll, relish, mustard. Use a thick slice of chocolate cream pie (better use boy versus boy or man versus man for this—girls don't like their faces messed up).

Be careful: Know your contestants for any stunt that might mess up clothes, faces or hands. Ask for volunteers. Don't allow any roughhousing. Provide a wet towel when the contest is over. Provide plastic cloth to cover clothes.

47. Going Steady

You'll need: An egg and a small paper or plastic spoon for each player. An open level area about 25 yards long. A rope about 20 inches high anchored across the middle of the area. Starting line. Finish line. A starter. A judge for the finish line.

What to do: Line up the couples behind the starting line, with inside elbows locked; outside arms held straight out, with hands holding the egg in the bowl of the small spoon. At the signal, each couple goes as fast as possible toward the finish line, trying not to drop the eggs. If an egg is dropped, the couple is eliminated. In the middle of the course they must step over that 20-inch-high rope. Couples must not unlock inner arms. Couples judged for first, second and third place.

Prizes: Chit for omelet at the corner drugstore. Tickets to the movie. China egg. Ceramic hen or rooster. Blue, white and red ribbons.

Variations: Use plastic eggs. Permit couple to pick up an egg if it is dropped, replace it on spoon and continue. Use lighted candles instead of egg-in-spoon.

Be careful: If uncooked eggs are used, collect them at once. Don't tempt the losers!

48. Slip Up

You'll need: A pie pan or flat dish for each partner. A cake of *wet* laundry soap in each plate. A table knife for each player. Two lines, about 15 feet apart. A judge to pick the winners.

What to do: Place partners facing each other, one on each line. Put pan with knife and bar of wet soap on line by each person. On signal, each partner tries to pick up and balance the bar of wet soap on the blade of the knife, walk with it to his partner's plate and deposit the soap into that plate. If soap slips off the knife, player must stop and get it back on the knife before going on (no fair spearing the soap). First couple to exchange the soap wins.

Prizes: Cake of soap for the woman, shaving cream for the man.

Be careful: Make sure the soap is slippery-wet. Knife must not pierce the soap.

49. TRAINED SEAL

You'll need: One or more couples. A lollipop and five rubber jar rings for each couple. Judges to select the winner.

What to do: Each man sits on the ground with legs crossed and hands flat on the ground at his side or slightly back of him. He holds the lollipop in his mouth, stick as straight up as possible. His partner stands on a line about six feet away. She throws the jar rings, one at a time, trying to ring the lollipop stick. Couple with the most ringers wins.

Prizes: Set of horseshoes or quoits. A gilded horseshoe. Pair of toy flippers.

Variations: One man can hold the lollipop stick while a line of women take turns in throwing the five jar rings, woman with the most ringers wins. Play as a father-son, father-daughter couple contest. Woman holds clothespin in her mouth while man tries to ring it with the jar rings.

Be careful: Players holding the target should remove eyeglasses before contest.

50. POTATO POLO (SEE ACTIVITY 36)

You'll need: Any number (six is good) of "horses" and "riders." A sharp-pointed stick for each rider. Three potatoes for each couple. A starting line.

What to do: Riders mount their horses behind starting lines. Each horse races on hands and knees to his pile of three potatoes about 30 feet away. The rider spears one potato at a time and rides back to the starting line with it. First horse and rider to bring back all three potatoes wins the polo match (horse may not touch the potatoes). Encourage horses to neigh, etc.

Prizes: Toy pony. Candy corn. Candy bars. Apples and sugar lumps for horses.

Variations: Reverse the roles for second relay (horse becomes rider and does the spearing). Use as a father-son contest, with Dad being the horse.

Be careful: This is hard on "horse's" knees, so keep the distance fairly short. Collect the spears and potatoes. When small children are the "riders," use wooden spoons to push each potato back to the starting line.

51. DRY UP

You'll need: Several couples. A glass of water and two spoons for each couple. String to tie the two spoons together, leaving about six inches between.

What to do: Give each couple a glass of water and two tied-together spoons. At signal they must spoon out and drink the water. Couple emptying their cup and spilling the least wins.

Prizes: A package of soda straws. Soft drinks. Package of powdered drink mix.

Variations: Try this with Jello, ice cream, cereal and milk. Or have each player spoon into his partner's mouth, not his own.

Be careful: Provide baby bibs or paper towel bibs for spills. Collect all equipment and clean up any spills.

INSTANT

PICNIC

LAUGH AND

chapter 6

CHEER MAKERS

Here are the Show-Stoppers, the Scene-Stealers, the Laugh-Makers, the Hold-Your-Breath Activities that no good picnic should be without. They become the Remember-Whens. "Remember when we won the tug-of-war?" "I'll never forget Bill's face with that chocolate ice cream all over it." "Remember when Laura won the baby-calling contest?" Those are Red Letter Events that make the picnic Something Special.

Many of the events in preceding chapters can become Specials if you play up the suspense and laughter. These are the two big ingredients: suspense, with its delicious combination of anticipation and fear; laughter, with its healing relief from tension. Provide them and your picnic's made.

52. NIAGARA FALLS

You'll need: A smooth, level playing area. Plenty of room along the sides for spectators. Volunteer players and a partner for each. Four- or five-inch balloons filled with water and securely tied. Referees to keep the playing lines straight and to eliminate players. Towels for mopping.

What to do: Partners line up, facing each other, about four feet away. Players on one line are each given a water balloon. At signal, each tosses the balloon to his partner. If a balloon drops, or breaks, both partners are OUT. The line now with the balloons steps back two steps and waits. At signal, the players toss the balloons to their partners. Again partners are eliminated if their balloon is dropped or breaks. The line with the balloons steps back another two steps, at signal the balloons are tossed again, and the contest continues, halting after each throw to straighten the lines and increase the throwing distance. Final couple to have unbroken balloon is winner.

Prize: A towel to cry in!

Variation: When the contest has been reduced to one couple, they toss the water balloon back and forth, taking two steps back after each throw, until finally one of them drops or breaks the balloon.

Be careful: This is exciting to watch. Keep spectators out of splash range. Be sure contestants wear suitable clothes. Best to limit this to boys and men, although women at a beach picnic might like to try it.

53. Egg Throw

You'll need: Same setup as Niagara Falls, but with an egg for each couple to toss. This is a Favorite Picnic Spectacular.

What to do: Follow directions for Niagara Falls. Signal for a stop after each throw, even up the lines, and increase distance by the line holding the eggs stepping back. All throws on signal only.

Prizes: A hen. A basket of eggs. A box of deviled eggs. Chit for an omelet in a local restaurant.

Variations: Announce that one of the eggs is hard-boiled. Announce that all the eggs may or may not be hard-boiled.

Be careful: Use only volunteers for this laugh-maker. Be sure players are suitably dressed. Keep the spectators out of splash range.

54. Cool It

You'll need: A setup very similar to Niagara Falls and Egg Throw. An ice cube for each couple.

What to do: Line up the partners facing each other about 10 feet apart. Give ice cubes to the players in one line. At signal partners begin tossing their ice cube back and forth. If their ice cube falls to the ground, or gets melted, the couple is eliminated. Last couple left with an ice cube is cool, man, cool! The WINNAH!

Prizes: Ice-cold soft drink. Ticket for a soda at the local drugstore.

Variations: The two players left in the game keep on tossing the ice cube, but stepping back on each throw until one of them fails to catch and hold it—last player wins. Try this contest using a lemon.

Be careful: Keep spectators out of splash range. Provide mop-up towel.

55. BARREL BOXING

You'll need: Barrels large enough for each contestant to stand in. A smooth, level, grassy area (if possible). Two pairs of large size boxing gloves or two newspaper swatters.

What to do: Place the barrels about two feet apart (sparring distance apart, depending upon size of contestants). Each boxer gets into a barrel. They box, trying to make each other fall out of the barrel.

Prizes: Miniature boxing gloves. Tin keg of cookies. Toy barrel bank.

Variations: Boxers stand on wooden boxes; each spars with the other and tries to make the other step down. Tie gloves securely to long sticks or broom handles, place boxes farther apart; players joust to make each other step down.

Be careful: Make sure contestants are evenly matched in weight and height. Make sure ground is free of glass or other litter. Provide gym mats or heavy tarpaulins to soften falls. If boxes are used, make sure the boxing gloves or other heavy padding is fastened securely.

56. EYE-TO-EYE

You'll need: Several couples. A dish of chocolate ice cream and a spoon for each person.

What to do: Players lie flat on their stomachs, partners' bodies stretching in opposite directions, their heads close together. Each player must feed his partner. First prize goes to the fastest and cleanest team.

Prizes: Washcloth. Package of paper towels. Chit for quart of ice cream at the local drugstore.

Variations: Use Jello instead of ice cream. Use small bag of popcorn. Have partners stretch out parallel to each other, on their sides, faces close together, ice cream in bowls about six inches from top of their heads.

Be careful: Provide wet towel for face cleaning. Make sure players are suitably dressed for this messy but funny contest. Provide plastic covers if necessary. Clean up the area when the contest is over.

57. BABY CALLING

You'll need: A smooth, grassy circle about 20 feet in diameter, marked off with rope, tape or chalk. Mothers with babies at the crawling stage. Judge to select first three children to cross the circle line.

What to do: All mothers place their crawlers in the center of the circle, then step back quickly to edge of the circle. Mothers coax their tots to crawl to them—rattles, balls, etc., allowed, but not inside the circle.

Prize: Blue, white and red ribbons. Baby harness. Big sign saying CHAMP. Knee patches for crawler's overalls.

Variations: Set up the area in lanes—crawlers at one end, mothers at other. Mothers coax the babies to crawl down the lane to the finish line.

Be careful: Make sure the playing area is entirely free from sticks, stones, glass or other objects that might scratch or be put in the mouth. Use a big tarpaulin for safety's sake. Any child who gets frightened or upset should be taken out at once. Give some sort of award to each baby.

58. WHISTLE STOP

You'll need: Four or more contestants. A whistle for each. A judge to pick the winner.

What to do: Line up the "blower-louds" about a foot apart, where everyone can see and hear them. Assign judges to listen closely. At signal each starts blowing the whistle. Player who whistles the longest wins.

Prize: A whistle. A toy drum or other musical instrument. A pair of ear stoppers or earmuffs. A cold drink.

Variations: Run in heats, four blowers at a time, then let winners compete. Play with men, then women; winning man and woman compete in final contest.

Be careful: Make sure judges eliminate any player making no sound—no pretending! Don't allow anyone with asthma or any sort of heart trouble to try this.

59. ORANGE PICKER

You'll need: An orange and two plastic tablespoons for each player. Judges to decide winners.

What to do: Pair up the players. Each holds an orange on a tablespoon in the right hand, and another tablespoon in the left hand. The two players joust or fence with each other. Each tries to upset the other's orange by using his free spoon—and at the same time keep his own orange from being knocked off.

Prizes: Cold orange drink. Orange-flavored candies. Orange cake.

Variations: Play as individual contest, the winner taking on a new challenger. Start five or six jousts at once, playing inside a circle about 20 feet in diameter, those dropping oranges eliminated until only one "orange picker" is left.

60. Hog Calling

You'll need: At least half a dozen, hopefully more, volunteer hog callers. Judges (pick them from the most eminent men or women of the town, or ask the entire group of spectator-listeners to act as judges). Set up the highest standards of hog calling—get a good emcee to announce these points.

What to do: Ahead of time, select the judges and brief the emcee. The emcee announces the points on which the callers will be scored, keeping them humorous. Conduct the contest with great ceremony, scoring points!

1. Volume, loudness and carrying quality of the voice, 30 points.
   (Suppose the hogs are in the back eighty and the wind is blowing in the wrong direction.)
2. Enticement or appeal to the hog, 20 points.
   (The voice should show sincerity and carry conviction to the hog.)

3. Originality, 10 points.
    (The hog wants to be able to identify his master's voice.)

4. Variety, 20 points.
    (Hogs like interesting calls. They are easily bored.)

5. Musical quality, 10 points.
    (Happy hogs will come a-running. They enjoy music, usually happy music.)

6. Appearance and facial expression, 10 points.
    (Hogs like to be proud of their owners. Owners should show that they like their hogs.)

Prizes: A piggy bank. A megaphone. Toy pig. Package of bacon.

Be careful: An "oldie" like this needs a light touch. Get some old-timers to volunteer. Keep the contest amusing but don't "ham" it too much. Best used at a large community picnic.

61. CHICKEN CALLING

You'll need: Somewhat the same setup as for the Hog Calling Contest, but use women instead of men.

What to do: Get women volunteers and a good emcee. Specify rating system:

1. Carrying capacity of voice, 25 points.
2. Musical quality, cadence, etc., 20 points.

3. Action and general appearance when scattering the food, 35 points.
4. Originality and variety of call, 20 points.

Prizes: Live hen. Chicken pie. Toy chicken. Candy corn.

Be careful: Keep it light. Encourage dramatic action. Make sure audience is laughing *with,* not *at* the contestants.

62. CALLING ALL MEN!

You'll need: Women for callers. A good emcee. Several judges.

What to do: Introduce the idea and the emcee. The emcee explains that husband callers will be judged on:

1. Voice appeal. How much "come hither" does it have?
2. Loudness. After all, husband may be a block away or sound asleep in front of the TV.
3. Facial expression. Does it add emphasis to the voice? Will it lure, not frighten him away?
4. Softness. Can she make husband hear, and yet not wake up the baby?

Prizes: Toy walkie-talkie. Megaphone. Toy telephone. Whistle.

Variations: Narrow the number down to several women. Have judges ask for another sample, letting the audience choose the winner by length of clapping. Try with teen-age girls calling their boy friends.

Be careful: Keep this sort of contest light, amusing and good-natured. Don't let it embarrass anyone.

63. Driving the Pigs to Market

You'll need: Relay teams of around five players each. A yardstick, broom handle, or stick for each team. A pop bottle, rounded glass milk bottle, duck pin or other object that won't roll straight. A level playing area. A starting line. A goal line about 20 to 25 feet away. Judge to select the winner.

What to do: Line each team up behind its captain (player number 1). Give each captain a yardstick. Place the "pig" on the starting line. At the signal, each captain must push his "pig" to the goal line, then "drive" it back to the starting line. He then gives the stick to player number 2 and goes to the end of his line. Player number 2 drives his pig to market and back. And so on until one team has driven all its pigs to market and back again.

Prize: Piggy bank. Package of bacon. Toy pig. Bag of new pennies. Bag of candy coins.

Variations: Play as individual races. Play men versus women. Play with mixed teams. Play husbands versus wives.

64. Powder Puffer

You'll need: Six or eight volunteers. For each player a pie plate which holds one unshelled peanut, covered with at least a half inch of flour. Starting line. Goal line about 30 feet away. Judges to select the winners.

What to do: Arrange the pie plates on the goal line, a plate directly in front of each player. At signal each player runs to his plate, gets down on hands and knees, blows off the flour, grabs the peanut in his teeth, and runs back with it to the starting line. He cannot touch the plate with his hands. First player back to the starting line wins.

Prize: Roll of paper towels. Clothes brush. Bag of peanuts. Nut candy bar.

Be careful: Provide someone to brush off the face and clothes. Dry towel for cleanup. Collect the pans and sweep up the flour.

65. FOUR CORNER TUG-OF-WAR

You'll need: Four evenly matched boys or men. A half-inch rope (sash cord can be used) about 25 feet long. Four stones, blocks or bean bags. Roped-off area to keep spectators out of the way.

What to do: Tie the two ends of the rope together securely. Lay the rope on the ground in the form of a square (keep the knot away from a corner). Place a boy or man at each corner. Place the stones, bean bags or other small objects diagonally out from each corner, about 10 feet behind each player. At signal the four players take up the rope. At second signal each tries to pull the others in such a way that he can reach his stone and pick it up. First

player to do so wins. Play two out of three, or three out of five trials.

Prizes: Pair of work gloves. Blue ribbon. Box of Wheaties (breakfast of champions!). *Superman* comic book. Hand lotion.

Be careful: This contest is interesting to watch but it can be rough. Make sure the players are evenly matched, especially in weight. Play on a soft or grassy area because there'll be spills.

66. TUG-OF-WAR

You'll need: A rope, at least ¾ inch thick and 40 feet long. A handkerchief or piece of white cloth tied in the exact middle of the rope and dangling in plain sight. Six or eight players on each team. A center line. Plenty of room.

What to do: Players on each team hold their side of the rope at one-foot intervals. The handkerchief should dangle exactly over the center line. At signal, each team tries to tug the other team completely over the center line. Play two out of three trials.

Prize: Work gloves. Bottle of hand lotion. Jump rope. Lariat. Blue ribbon. Candy bars.

Variations: Play married versus unmarried men. Play with a time limit, team farthest away from center line when whistle blows being the winner. Play two out of three, changing sides. For special groups on special occasions, water the center area until it is muddy.

Be careful: Tug-of-War can be rough. Girls and women sometimes take part (never against boys and men) but don't include them unless you know the group very well. Use on soft or grassy area because there will be spills. Use the mud-center type of Tug-of-War with caution—parents sometimes object to muddy clothes!

si frankel

INSTANT

chapter 7

PICNIC THEMES

Themes are ways of making a picnic (or party) hang together. They are topics that suggest specific decorations, foods, possibly costumes, prizes and activities. The nice thing about themes is that everybody gets involved. He or she must rise to the occasion, devise a costume, perhaps, and be ready to join in the activities that the theme requires. Themes establish a festive atmosphere.

Use themes as interest-arousers and to suggest decorations, but keep them under control. Don't let the theme become so important that it runs the picnic.

Themes, of course, should be selected in terms of the group. Spacemen might intrigue young boys, but their parents probably would prefer a Hawaiian or South American fiesta theme. In some cases, the theme only sets the stage and supplies the motif for the picnic—Japanese lanterns can turn a back yard or Village Green into a fairyland—while the food and the activities are strictly American plan. Often the decorations and background music carry out the theme pretty well without pushing it too hard.

Holidays and special days always make good themes, and activities suitable for various age levels fit nicely into such themes. Independence Day, July 4, is a perfect example. In general, a good rule to remember is that the larger the group, the more general the theme should be. A community Fourth of July picnic would feature patriotic music; red, white and blue decorations; perhaps a parade. But it might include water sports, races, relays, fireworks, a speech or two—something for everybody.

Themes for large groups are like umbrellas, broad enough to cover everybody. For small groups they can become more like spotlights, focusing attention to specific plans.

The nine themes that follow are suggestions only, intended to show that a theme can be used for a small, neighborhood picnic or expanded to add color and life to a large affair. Hundreds of other themes are possible: birthdays of famous people; dates of important events (or the events themselves); holidays; special days such as Mother's Day, Father's Day, April Fools' Day, etc.

Picnics don't really need any excuse or reason. They have the three magic and basic ingredients: People, Eating, Program—in one word, P E P. Remember?

* * * *

67. PIRATE PICNIC

Decorations: skull and crossbones on posters, black and white pennants, cardboard daggers wrapped in silver foil.

Dress: eye patches (open space for eye to see through), bandannas or headbands, big gold earrings (brass curtain rings).

Treasure chest (big box wrapped in brown paper, decorated with gold paint): to hold prizes for the activities or a special treat (candy coin money wrapped in foil, in gilt bags; a watermelon; ice cream; lollipops).

Treasure hunt, with clues on a pirate map of buried treasure.

Games adapted to pirate theme: Peg-leg Race (three-legged race); Walk the Plank (walking a balance beam, or a straight line, but using the wrong end of opera glasses or binoculars); Capture the Flag (like Potato Race).

For older groups: treasure hunt or scavenger hunt, campfire cooking, dancing, talent show, folk singing.

68. South American Fiesta

Lots of colors, all bright: green, red, yellow, blue.

Flags of Central and South American nations.

Music: tangos, sambas, cha-chas, rumbas; strolling guitar, accordion or banjo players.

Gay dress: full skirts, lots of beads, earrings for the girls; bright sashes, gay shirts, blue jeans for the boys.

Strolling vendors: with balloons, hot dogs, noisemakers—for sale or giveaway.

Dance: contests, folk dancing by special group.

Piñata scramble for the small-fry.

Games and races adapted to the theme: rodeos, cowboys, bullfighters.

69. Aloha Picnic

Flares and torches, if fire safety permits.

Girls and women in muu-muus (long, shapeless dresses,

usually gaily printed with big, bright flowers), flowers in hair, leis around neck.

Boys and men in gay shirts, shorts, blue jeans, flowers behind ears, leis around neck.

Hawaiian music on the record player or over the public address system, steel guitar player.

Hula contests: real for women, comic for men.

Luau feast served on wooden plates (or simulated), cocoanut juice (milk) for the youngsters, pineapple drinks.

Beach games and contests (in pool, if available).

Leis for prizes.

70. GYPSY PICNIC

Red lanterns, colored spotlights, or real campfires for lighting.

Girls or women in long, full skirts, lots of beads, earrings, bracelets, ankle bells. Hair in braids or loose.

Boys or men in bright shirts, bandannas, slouch hats, artificial mustaches, earring in one ear, bright sashes, blue jeans.

Fortune teller—in tent, or strolling around.

Accordion, violin or guitar player strolling around. Or gypsy music on the record player.

Campfire cooking, by individuals or on larger scale.

Campfire singing. Dancing.

Games and contests adapted to theme: horseback (stick horses) races, cock fights (dual contests).

71. BALLOON BASH

Easy! Useful for pool picnics, too.

Balloons of all sizes, shapes and colors.

Balloon games and contests: batting balloons, pushing balloons, fanning balloons, breaking balloons, painting balloons, carrying balloons.

72. Japanese Picnic

Pretty, and simple for a friend-and-neighbor picnic.

Japanese lanterns, flowers, pine branches for decorations. Fans for everybody. Women and girls in kimonos if they like.

Guests sit on ground to eat, with or without low tables. Chopsticks.

Serve sukiyaki or other Japanese dishes: rice, tea, fortune cookies.

Use chopsticks for stunt feeding contests. Use fans to propel Ping-Pong ball or balloon.

73. Celestial Picnic

Similar to Theme 72. Decorate paper tableclothes by painting Chinese characters (or your variations!) with red ink or poster paint.

Guests can come in "coolie" costume: blue denim trousers, mid-calf length; loose shirts and smocks; sandals; fans.

Chow mein, chop suey, egg rolls, tea, kumquats, lichee nuts. Chopsticks.

Kite flying, if area permits.

Fireworks, if law allows.

74. Beach Picnic

This event can be seaside, lakeside, or poolside. Water, if available for water games, will be the chief attraction.

Games and races involving beachballs. Volleyball. Sand sculpturing contests. Sand castle building. Board games using sand as the board, pebbles or shells as the "men."

Open-fire or pit-cooked meals. Regional specialties such as clambake, barbecues. Box lunches.

Guests come by car; or hike; or bicycle. Picnic by sunshine or moonlight. Combines nicely with a pirate or beachcomber theme.

75. CIRCUS OR CARNIVAL PICNIC

Lots of volunteer clowns. Makeup to change the faces of youngsters into clowns, Indians, Orientals, mustached villains.

Lots of balloons, cotton candy, peanuts, funny hats, masks, pennants, noisemakers.

Games and races for all age groups. Ringmaster for judge or emcee. Wiener or hamburger booths, soft drinks, hot coffee, ice cream. Tables and benches for the bring-your-own lunchers.

Band music. Pony rides. Carrousel. Puppet show. Magicians. Band concert and street dance in the evening.

RESOURCES

Manuals, Bulletins, Book Lists, Books

• Public Library. Look through books of active games, contests, stunts.

• Local municipal and county recreation and/or park agency. Ask for any manuals, game bulletins, etc., on picnic activities.

• The National Recreation and Park Association, 7100 Pennsylvania Avenue, N.W., Washington, D.C. 20006. Ask for book lists and suggestions for picnic activities.

Maps, Directories, Information on Site and Facilities

• Local municipal and county recreation and park agencies. Most of them issue attractive directories and other information.

• Your state, especially its department of parks, conservation, and commerce. Ask for maps and directories of public and private picnic areas and facilities.

• The National Park Service of the U.S. Department of the Interior and the Forestry Division of the U.S. Department of Agriculture. Ask for maps and directories for picnic sites and facilities in National Parks and Forests in whatever region you wish.

INFORMATION ON INDUSTRIAL PICNICS

(No prices are given here, because they are subject to change. Write for information about price and availability.)
- *Employee Picnics.* Industrial Recreation Association, 1 North La Salle Street, Chicago 2, Illinois.
- *Let's Have a Picnic.* Organization Services, Inc., 8259 Livernois, Detroit 4, Michigan.

SOURCES FOR NOVELTY PRIZES, DECORATIONS, FLAGS

(These are only a few and should be supplemented by using the Yellow Pages of your telephone directory for local or nearby sources.)
- Academy Carnival Equipment Co., 39 Union Square, West, New York, New York. A source for carnival-type equipment, appropriate mostly for very large picnics.
- Annin & Co., 85 Fifth Avenue, New York, New York. Sources for flags of all sizes and all nations.
- Brok & Co., 133 North Third Street, Reading, Pennsylvania. Source for novelty toys and party favors.
- Organization Services, Inc., 8259 Livernois, Detroit 4, Michigan. Source for equipment and novelty prizes for large picnics of the industrial type.
- B. Shackman & Co., 2 West 35th Street, New York, New York. Toys, novelties, party favors.
- United Nations Gift Shop, United Nations Plaza, New York, New York. Small flags of all nations, gifts, toys.
- Wright Studios, 5264 Brookville Road, Indianapolis, Indiana 46219. Novelties, decorations, many with an international theme.